My Little Golden Book About
Boston

By Judy Katschke
Illustrated by Melanie Demmer

A GOLDEN BOOK • NEW YORK

Educators and librarians, for a variety of teaching tools, visit us at RHTeachersLibrarians.com
Library of Congress Control Number: 2021947490
ISBN 978-0-593-47940-7 (trade) — ISBN 978-0-593-47941-4 (ebook)
Printed in the United States of America
10 9 8 7 6 5 4 3 2 1

Hi! I'm Beanie the Boston Terrier. I'm one lucky dog because I live in **Boston**, Massachusetts. Want to know what makes my city so *wicked awesome*? Follow me!

Hear ye! Hear ye! Our first stop is **Faneuil Hall**. This is the public meeting space where George Washington made a toast to celebrate America's first birthday. Speeches are still made inside.

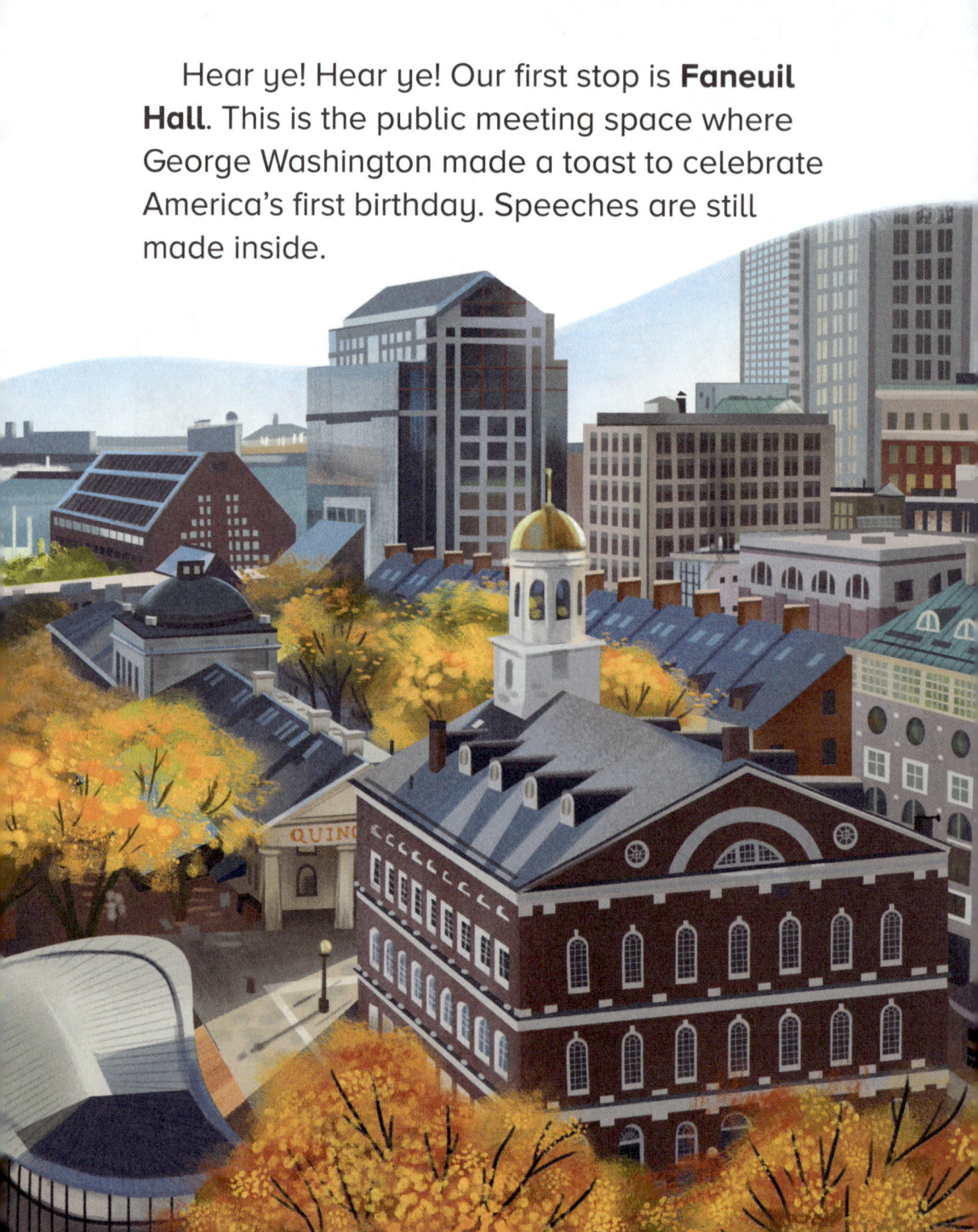

Outside it's a quick walk to **Quincy Market**. Here you can watch performers, buy souvenirs, and get snacks from hundreds of food stands and pushcarts. May I suggest the Boston clam *chowdah*?

Next let's check out **Fenway Park**, home of the Boston Red Sox. A ride on the T, the local subway train, will speed us to the baseball stadium and its famous left-field wall, known as the Green Monster!

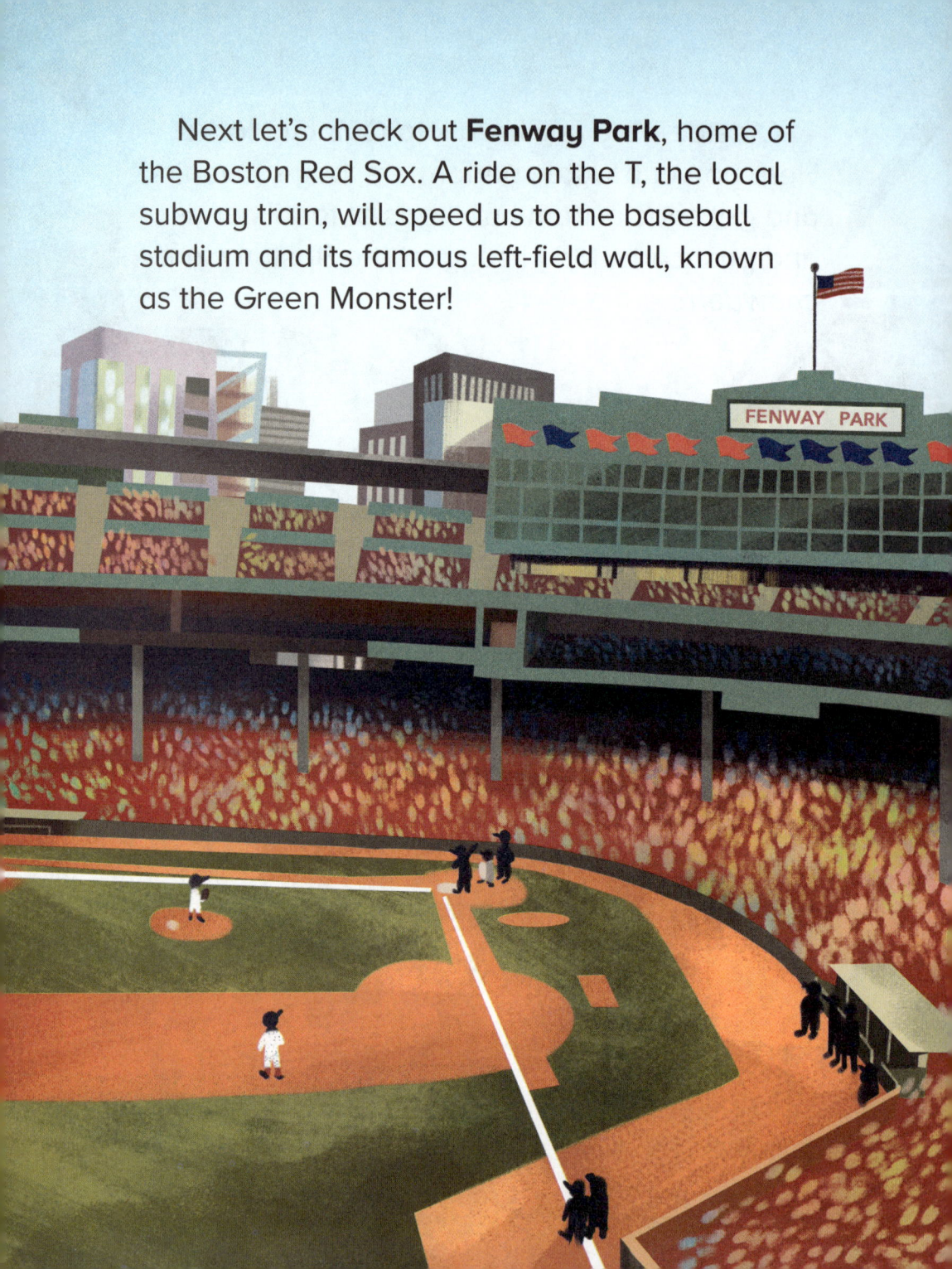

My VIP (Very Informed Pup) tour continues with the **Greenway Carousel**. Instead of the usual horses, this carousel lets you ride on animals from the Boston area, such as an owl, a sea turtle, a fox, and a lobster.

Time to follow the red brick road along Boston's **Freedom Trail**. With sixteen American Revolution sites, history is no mystery here! Drop by **Paul Revere's House**, the oldest building in Boston.

Or ask a guide to show you the **Old Corner Bookstore**, where America's first books were printed.

Don't forget to look for the statue of Benjamin Franklin in front of **Old City Hall**. He's a favorite with visitors—and the occasional pigeon!

There's nothing common about **Boston Common**! The oldest city park in the United States is where you'll find the **Frog Pond**. Once filled with croaking frogs, the pond is now filled with floating carved pumpkins in the fall, used as a splashy spray pool each summer, and enjoyed as a skating rink during the winter. Whatever the season, the Frog Pond is hopping with fun!

Now let's hop over to the **Franklin Park Zoo**. Here you can see lions, giraffes, wildebeests, and even a hissing cockroach. After visiting the animals, you can pretend to be one and climb in the zoo's 10,000-square-foot playground, just like a ring-tailed lemur. Yup, the zoo has lemurs, too!

Our next *fin*-tastic stop is the **New England Aquarium**, home to thousands of sea creatures. Gaze into the four-story Giant Ocean Tank to watch lionfish, sea turtles, and eels swim by.

Chill with rockhopper penguins, and then enter the jiggly world of sea jellies. If hands-on fun is what you want, dig into the aquarium's Touch Tank to pet a ray or an epaulette shark.

It's on to **Boston's Waterfront**, where you can hike or bike for miles along the water's edge. Take a whiff of the salty sea air—or the tasty treats from hundreds of food trucks and restaurants! I recommend getting a frosty Boston frappe (that's what locals call a milkshake).

From the waterfront, you can catch a ride on a tall sailing ship or count whales from the deck of a whale-watching cruise boat. *Thar she blows!*

A quick ferry ride will take us from the waterfront to **Boston Harbor Islands**. Each island has its own treasure, like a Civil War fort to explore, a lighthouse to climb, or a sandy beach to enjoy.

To protest a tea tax, colonists in 1773 stormed three ships and dumped chests of tea into Boston Harbor. This brings us to our next adventure, the **Boston Tea Party Ships & Museum**.

Here costumed actors and holograms share exciting stories of the historical midnight raid. Check out one of the only two surviving tea chests, then climb aboard an eighteenth-century vessel and toss tea into the harbor!

With hundreds of dinosaur bones, the **Harvard Museum of Natural History** is a dog's dream come true. Humans *dig* it, too, because there's so much to see.

You can examine million-year-old fossils, exotic birds, and glittery gemstones.

There's *swan* more place to go on our tour!
Boston Public Garden blooms with thousands of
beautiful flowers and trees in the spring. It's also
where you can cruise the lagoon on Boston's
world-famous swan boats.

Seeing so many *wicked-cool* sights in just one day can make a pup dog-tired. I hope you'll visit me in Boston again someday so we can do it all again!